A Gift for
the ~~best~~
Library
Media Center
from
~~Benjamin Gyi~~
on his
9th birthday
October 28, 1996

Chibi

A True Story from Japan

by Barbara Brenner and Julia Takaya
Illustrated by June Otani

Clarion Books
New York

Clarion Books
a Houghton Mifflin Company imprint
215 Park Avenue South, New York, NY 10003
Text copyright © 1996 by Barbara Brenner and Julia Takaya
Illustrations copyright © 1996 by June Otani

Illustrations executed in watercolor and ink on Arches hot-press watercolor paper.
Text is 13/18-point New Aster.

For information about this and other Houghton Mifflin trade and reference books
and multimedia products, visit The Bookstore at Houghton Mifflin on the
World Wide Web at (http://www.hmco.com./trade/).

Printed in Singapore.

Library of Congress Cataloging-in-Publication Data

Brenner, Barbara.
Chibi : a true story from Japan / by Barbara Brenner and Julia Takaya ; illustrated by June Otani.
p.   cm.
ISBN 0-395-69623-2
1. Chibi (Duck)—Juvenile literature. 2. Spotbill duck—Japan—Tokyo—Biography—Juvenile literature.
3. Japan—Social life and customs—Juvenile literature. [1. Chibi (Duck) 2. Spotbill duck. 3. Ducks.
4. Japan—Social life and customs.] I. Takaya, Julia. II. Otani, June, ill. III. Title.
QL696.A52B735 1995
598.4'1—dc20   94-31082
CIP
AC
TWP   10 9 8 7 6 5 4 3 2 1

To Cousin Kate—B.B.
To my mother, who said, Use your life—J.T.

To my cousins—
Ritsuko, Hiroko, and Yoshiko—J.O.

Chapter 1

One spring morning a brown-and-gold duck flew over a skyscraper in Tokyo, Japan.

Far below her she spied a pool of water gleaming like glass. She dipped down and glided onto it, hardly making a splash. After a quick look around, the duck settled down in a clump of ivy by the pool and proceeded to build her nest.

It didn't seem to bother her that she was in an office park in downtown Tokyo . . . or that she was only a stone's throw away from Uchibori *Dori,* the eight-lane avenue where three hundred cars a minute roar in and out of the city. The duck went right on with her work.

Soon the nest held ten ivory-colored eggs. The *oka-san* brooded them herself, turning the eggs gently with her feet from time to time so they would keep warm on all sides.

Twenty-six days later there was a commotion in the ivy. One egg cracked, and a wet little baby duck pecked its way out of the shell. Then another egg hatched, then seven more. Within hours there were nine fluffy ducklings in the ivy, snuggled under their mother's warm brood feathers.

It seemed as if the tenth egg might be a dud. But on the next day it finally cracked open and a very small and scraggly duckling pushed out of the shell. Oka-san patiently moved the other ducklings about in the nest to make room for this last and tiniest member of the family.

As soon as number ten was fluffed out and steady on her feet, the mother duck led her entire brood out of the nest and onto the ledge above the pool.

That was when the workers in the offices in Mitsui Office Park saw the ducks for the first time. The ducks caused a sensation. Word spread like wildfire. *Eleven wild* kamo *are living around the pool!*

People began to visit the park just to watch the duck family and to take pictures of them. Among the duck watchers was a news photographer, Mr. Sato, who gave a name to the tiniest duckling. Sato-san named her *Chibi,* which means "tiny."

Every day the crowd grew larger. People brought lunch in their kerchiefs to eat beside the pool so they could watch Oka-san and her ducklings. Vendors moved in with hot-noodle carts, carts of *oden* (steamed vegetables) and *isobe maki* (rice cakes wrapped in seaweed) and with ice-cream and cake carts.

Tokyo TV started to broadcast a "Duck Watch" on the evening news. School children came on class trips to see the *kamo* family. Photographers came to take pictures. Sato-san was there every day.

Soon four thousand people a day were visiting the Mitsui Office Park to see Oka-san and her ducklings. Chibi was clearly their favorite. Everyone worried about her. Being the smallest and youngest, she struggled to catch up with her brothers and sisters, who had already learned Waddle, Line Up, Follow the Leader, and Belly-whopper Splash. When Chibi finally learned to dive under the water to get moss to eat, everyone celebrated. "Chibi! Chibi!" they chanted. Sato-san took the first pictures of Chibi "bottoms up."

One morning in June, Oka-san hastily quack-quacked the ducklings together. When they were all in a line, she marched them to one of the exits and right out of the office park! Sato-san and the other duck watchers trailed after her at a safe distance. When she reached the corner, Oka-san stopped short, turned, and waddled all the way back to the pool, her ducklings right behind her.

She repeated the trip seven times that morning.

"What is that crazy Oka-san doing?" people asked one another. Sato-san thought he knew. The duck family had outgrown the little pool at the office park. But right across the street was an ideal place for growing ducklings—the great moat in the Emperor's Gardens. Oka-san was going to take her family there. She was planning to cross Uchibori *Dori!*

But when? Nobody knew, not even Sato-san. The police were notified to be on the alert. They would stop traffic for the ducks. Sato-san and some of the other photographers brought sleeping bags and prepared to spend the night. Many of them had traveled a long way to capture on film the exciting moment when the *kamo* crossed the eight-lane avenue.

Night came, and lights went on in the city. The moon came out. Everything was quiet around the little pond. As dawn broke, the duck watchers listened for the first sounds of activity in the ivy. But the duck family slept on.

At eleven o'clock in the morning, Oka-san was still asleep, her head tucked under her wing. Chibi and the other ducklings were paddling around in the pool, chasing water spiders. Could it be that Mama Duck had changed her mind? Sato-san took out his shaver and freshened up a bit. He passed around a thermos of *ocha*. But the hot green tea couldn't take away the effects of a sleepless night. Some of the photographers decided to leave. Others dozed in their camp chairs and sleeping bags. To pass the time, Sato-san took pictures of his friends sleeping.

At exactly noon, the mother duck lifted her bill, stood up, and waggled her tail. Was the bill or the tail the signal? The ducklings gathered behind their mother—Chibi first, then the others. Marching single file, they followed Oka-san to the exit. But—wait! She wasn't leading them to where the watchers had gathered. Oka-san was heading for the *opposite* exit.

Sato-san was the first to realize what she meant to do. Frantically he dialed the police. Then, camera in hand, he clambered over the azalea bushes and raced along the divider to the other exit.

The street crossing light was changing from *midori* to *akai*—green to red. Oka-san ignored it. Looking straight ahead, she waddled down from the curb. Chibi and the other ducklings did the same. At that moment a sports car came speeding down the broad avenue. It was heading straight for the ducks. Sato-san, who was about to take a picture, dropped his camera and ran into the street. Waving his arms frantically, he shouted at the driver to stop. *"Tomatte! Tomatte!"*

The car swerved. Brakes screeched. Police whistles blew. Flashbulbs went off. But Oka-san paid no attention. Calmly she herded her brood across four lanes, up onto the divider, then down onto the remaining four lanes.

Within minutes the *kamo* family had crossed the wide avenue and had reached the other side safely.

Mama Duck flew down into the moat first. She paddled around, encouraging her family to join her. One by one they obeyed, tumbling over the steep rocky sides and plopping into the green water.

Only Chibi was left teetering on the edge of the high wall. She quacked mournfully. Her brothers and sisters were already swimming away from her with Oka-san, who seemed not to realize that Chibi had been left behind.

Sato-san called to the duckling. "Go on, Chibi, you can make it."

Now Oka-san turned back and swam toward Chibi, quacking anxiously. Chibi looked down at the water. It was far, far down. The top of the wall must have seemed as high as Mount Fuji to her. She gave one final quack and—

Splash! Chibi joined her family in the garden moat of the Emperor of Japan.

That night the front page of every Tokyo newspaper featured the duck story. Sato-san was disappointed that he hadn't gotten a picture of the *kamo* crossing Uchibori *Dori.* But he was happy that he was the one who had helped the duck family to cross the avenue safely.

Chapter 2

On his next visit, Sato-san saw that Chibi and her brothers and sisters were in a fine place for growing ducklings. The water was thick with green plants to eat, and there was plenty of space to practice flying.

However, the little *kamo* were not alone. Gold, red, and silver carp darted through the water. Square-headed turtles scavenged the bottom for bits of food, and dappled water snakes sunned themselves on the rocks. There were swans in the moat, too. The swans, the ducks discovered, were the least friendly of the creatures who shared the moat.

The swans would suddenly appear on the water like a fleet of white sailing ships. When the ducks were in their path they hissed and trumpeted in a terrifying way. Chibi had the hardest time keeping out of the swans' path. When she saw them coming, she would paddle as fast as her little webbed feet could go, to get out of the reach of their clapping beaks.

People continued to visit the duck family and to take pictures of them. There was always a crowd standing at the iron railing around the moat. Even joggers circling the gardens paused to have a look. Everyone knew Chibi. They worried with her when the swans got too close. Sato-san visited every day. He always had a special "Good day" for Chibi. "*Konnichi-wa,* Chibi," he would call, and his voice would echo off the rocks.

In June the rainy season arrived in Tokyo. There were gentle showers every day. Uchibori *Dori* was always slick and shiny with water. But Sato-san and the duck watchers still came to visit the ducks. They stood in puddles under their umbrellas, smiling at the sight of Chibi and her brothers and sisters playing in the raindrops.

Then came unusual weather. It began to rain harder and more steadily. Typhoons blew in almost every day. Powerful *kaze* drove the rain down in sheets and torrents. The wind also tore the branches from cherry trees and bent the willows until their leaves covered the ground. Sheets of rain pelted the surface of the moat, and the water was whipped into a sea of whitecaps.

Now only a few people braved the outdoors, and there was hardly a car on Uchibori *Dori*. Sato-san was worried about Chibi and the other ducks. He tried to fight his way against the wind to get to the moat, but after he was knocked off his feet he gave up and went home.

The moat began to fill up. Water poured over the spillway in an angry, foaming waterfall. Trees, roots, pieces of plastic, even the golden carp were washed over the edge and carried along with the rushing tide. It was a flood. The swans had long since left the water for high ground. They huddled together, their heads

tucked under their wings. The snakes had disappeared into crevices in the rocks. The turtles were safe on the muddy bottom of the moat, inside their shell houses.

But where were the *kamo?* That was the question in many people's minds. Sato-san sat in his apartment and worried about the ducks, especially about Chibi.

The storms went on for days and days. Then the rain stopped, the skies cleared, and people were able to go outside again. The duck watchers hurried to the Emperor's Gardens to look for the ducks. But there was no sign of them. Sato-san walked the whole length of the moat. At last he caught sight of Mama Duck. But she had only seven ducks with her. Three ducklings were missing—and one of them was Chibi.

Sato-san immediately organized a search party. People checked the moat from one end to the other, looking everywhere for footprints, feathers, bones— any clue to the disappearance of the young ducks. Even the Emperor's guards and gardeners joined the search. Meanwhile, Oka-san swam up and down, quacking frantically. When she failed to find her missing children on the water, she took to the air and flew along the banks and stone walls above the moat. Then she flew over Uchibori *Dori* to the Mitsui Office Park, where she searched the old nest in the ivy. But Chibi and the other two ducklings were nowhere to be seen.

Two days later, one of the ducklings was found—dead. It had been drowned in the flood. After the news was announced, hundreds of people brought fresh flowers and made a small shrine at the spillway, as a memorial to the drowned duckling. Sato-san took pictures of the shrine. He thought sadly of the other two missing ducks. If Chibi's larger brother had been caught by the force of the typhoon, what were the tiny duck's chances for survival?

The next morning, the second missing duck suddenly appeared. No one knew where it had been or how it had managed to find its way home. Yet there it was, seeming none the worse for wear. But where was Chibi?

Now something truly amazing happened. Sato-san heard loud quacking at the far end of the moat. He ran toward the sound. Oka-san heard it, too. She took off and flew in the same direction.

Before either of them reached the spot, a tiny figure floated into view. It was Chibi! She was balanced like a surfer on a piece of Styrofoam. Somehow the brave little duck had been able to stay afloat on the makeshift raft during the raging storm. The plastic had saved her life.

Click! Sato-san's camera captured the happy moment.

The story of Chibi's return, along with Sato-san's picture, was the front-page story in all the Tokyo papers. When the Emperor learned of the brave struggle of the *kamo* he ordered a special strong, handsome duck house built for them.

It stands there today, in the moat of the Imperial Gardens in Tokyo, Japan. Every year Chibi and her brothers and sisters come back to nest and to raise broods of their own. And if you ever visit there you may notice a certain elderly Japanese gentleman nearby, taking pictures.

Behind This Story

Chibi is based on a true story. Julia Takaya, an American teacher-writer who is married to a Japanese businessman, was among the thousands of Tokyo residents who followed the adventures of the brave mama duck attempting to raise her brood in the hubbub of the city. Like the photographers, the news media, and everyone else in the capital city, Julia Takaya fell under the spell of the ducks.

When she came back to the United States on a visit, she brought the story with her. She and writer Barbara Brenner agreed that the tale of tiny Chibi, the elderly photographer Mr. Sato, the Emperor's moat, and the flood was a timeless true story that children would enjoy.

A Few Additional Facts You Might Like to Know:

The duck in this story belongs to the species *Anas poecilorhyncha.* Its common name is the Spotbill Duck.

The Mitsui Company of Tokyo has put a duck house on the little pond in the office park for the returning ducks and their families.

Japanese word	Say it this way	It means
akai	*ah kah ee*	red
Chibi	*Chee bee*	tiny
dori	*doh ree*	street or avenue
isobe maki	*ee soh beh mah kee*	rice cakes usually wrapped in seaweed
kamo	*kah moh*	duck or ducks
kaze	*kah zeh*	wind or winds
konnichi-wa	*kon nee chee wah*	good day
midori	*mee doh ree*	green
ocha	*oh cha*	green tea
oden	*oh den*	steamed fish and vegetables
Oka-san	*Oh kah sahn*	Mother
Sato-san	*Sah toh sahn*	Sato is a last name San means respected (Mrs., Mr., or Miss)
tomatte	*toh mah teh*	stop

598.4
BRE   Brenner, Barbara   96-19

             Chibi

$14.95

DATE			
JA 7 '96			
MY 26 '98